THE LAST OF OLD EUROPE

A Grand Tour with
AJP TAYLOR

SIDGWICK & JACKSON
LONDON

First published in Great Britain in 1976
by Sidgwick and Jackson Limited
Introduction © AJP Taylor 1976
Photographs © Conway Picture Library 1976
First softcover edition 1984

Designed by Paul Watkins

Photographic Acknowledgments:
The photographs reproduced on pages 25, 29, 214,
215 and 223 are by permission of Andrew Mollo, and
those on pages 75 (top), 77 and 165 by permission of
the National Monuments Record. The remainder of
the photographs are from the collection of the
Conway Picture Library.

ISBN 0 283 99170 4

Printed in Great Britain by
A. Wheaton & Company Ltd, Exeter
for Sidgwick & Jackson Limited
1 Tavistock Chambers, Bloomsbury Way
London WC1A 2SG

Front endpapers: The King of Bulgaria driving in
state along Tergovska Street, Sofia
Back endpapers: Canal scene in Hamburg
Half-title: Fair on Hampstead Heath in London
Title pages: Happy days in the Sultan's harem
Opposite: Itinerant photographer in rural France

Contents

THE YEAR 1848 was of great moment in European history both as an end and as a beginning. It was the year of revolutions, the culmination of the political upheaval that had started with the French revolution of 1789. Every country on the continent of Europe was affected, Belgium less than the rest. Only the two countries on the fringes of Europe – Russia on the east and Great Britain across the Channel – were unshaken. In this Springtime of Nations everything seemed made anew. Absolute monarchies were challenged. Liberal constitutions were established. In France universal suffrage had its first triumph. Recognized nations, such as the German and the Italian, asserted their political rights. Nations hitherto unknown sprang into existence.

Within a year the revolutionary wave faltered and broke. In much of Europe the traditional order was restored, seemingly unchanged or even stronger than before. All that remained to outward appearance was a fairly liberal constitution in Piedmont – the Kingdom of Sardinia – a less liberal constitution in Prussia and a Bonaparte – later to become Napoleon III – instead of a Bourbon king as a ruler of France. No doubt the appearance was misleading. The ideas of Liberalism and Nationalism retained their force and were to achieve many successes in later years, though by less revolutionary means. But the great age of revolutions on the French model was over. There was none of any importance between 1848 and the end of the first world war except for the belated and comparatively unsuccessful Russian revolution of 1905. Even after the first world war, only the Bolshevik revolution had any basic significance. After the second world war there were no spontaneous revolutions at all in Europe except perhaps in Yugoslavia. The shadow of revolution often raised an alarm. It remained a spectre.

Yet 1848 marked much more a beginning than an end. This new revolution was less specific than the political turmoils that had preceded it. It was a change in men's beliefs, in their view of the universe and more prosaically in their way of life. Darwin was to shake men's confidence that they were a unique creation, only a little lower than the angels. Freud was to destroy men's conviction of their own rationality. Scientists ended the reign of Newton's immutable laws and substituted for them the principle of indeterminancy. Men lost their old security. At the same time they were free to believe there was no limit to what they could achieve if they set themselves to it. Men came to see themselves as lords of the universe just when they ceased to be lords of themselves.

The basis for this limitless and indeed grotesque confidence was to be found in British achievements during the preceding hundred years. The Industrial Revolution was Great Britain's individual contribution to civilization, a process that had no precise beginning and in a sense has had no end, but a revolution all the same. For the first time since the invention of the wheel men increased their physical power. Until 1830 motive forces were men themselves, draught animals – horses or oxen – and occasionally wind and water. Suddenly machines driven by coal took the place of men and animals. Men could move faster and further. They could produce more. George Stephenson, inventor of the Rocket locomotive, took the place of Rousseau, author of *The Social Contract*, as the examplar for mankind. Great Britain, not France, became the European ideal, and the City of God was found in Manchester instead of in Rome or Paris. Textiles counted for more than the Rights of Man. Napoleon, the erstwhile conqueror of Europe, was overshadowed by the Napoleons of railway-building and finance.

Until the middle of the nineteenth century Great Britain led and the rest of Europe lagged behind. The Great Exhibition of 1851, the first of its kind, symbolized the future which Great Britain offered to the peoples of Europe and ultimately to the whole world. Many Europeans were eager to follow the British lead and did so in the subsequent half-century. The spread of this new economic order was not even. By the beginning of the twentieth century, Germany surpassed Great Britain as the greatest industrial power in Europe. Meanwhile such areas as the Balkans, southern Spain and southern Italy were hardly affected. For much of the period Russia was a by-word for backwardness, yet by the beginning of the twentieth century some of the largest and and most advanced industrial establishments were to be found in Russia, and the way was already clear for the developments that have made Soviet Russia the second greatest industrial power in the world.

Old and new were mixed together, sometimes side by side, sometimes overlapping. If we went back to the Europe of a century ago we should often feel at home. We should know how to buy a railway ticket, how to draw a cheque, how to put on our clothes and in what order. We could read a daily newspaper and send a telegram. On the other hand our driving lessons would not qualify us to drive or ride a horse. Once off the beaten track we should find men still living in primitive straw huts, making their own traditional clothes and sometimes dying of starvation. We should find men who

8

Oxen and ox driver

could not read and write and had no idea what state or nation they belonged to. We should find men who were respected for their hereditary rank instead of for their money. We should even find monarchs with absolute power of life and death.

Moreover even in the most revolutionary times many men do not notice what is happening although it is happening to themselves. During the great French revolution, for instance, a Scotch gardener, employed to tend the palace gardens in Paris, kept a regular diary. He never made any reference to political events except on 10 August 1793, when he noted that crowds had trampled on the flower beds at the Tuilleries. This was in fact the armed rising which led to the fall of the French monarchy. In much the same way there were throughout the later nineteenth century village communities following the styles of life they had always followed, while not far away men in cities already possessed many of the advantages which we regard as characteristically modern – electric light, indoor sanitation, telephones, speedy travel.

These sixty years of unprecedented change are more vivid for us than any that went before. Thanks to the invention of photography we can actually see them. Photography was itself a product of the age. Though it did not depend on factories or steam power, it had some connection with science, an essential characteristic of the time. Also, perhaps, it derived partly from the increasing desire for information, a characteristic shown in the wider circulation of newspapers. The photographs of this time were stills in a literal sense. They needed a five-minute exposure and thus were spoilt by any considerable movement. Hence the earlier photographers preferred city streets when they were almost empty. In the same way the human subjects were clearly posed. We should not suppose that they were equally immobile in real life. On the contrary, men were on the move as they had never been before.

Karl Marx was fond of quoting the Greek philosopher Democritus: Παντα ῥεῖ, all things change. Change and movement were the dominant features of the age. There were changes in men's minds, changes in their way of life and changes in where they lived. The change in ideas is the one most difficult to illustrate. Photographs show devout congregations attending their village churches as they had always done; other photographs remind us that as many churches were built during the nineteenth century as in the Middle Ages. Nevertheless the proportion of believers steadily decreased, and many of those who still called themselves Christians did not believe in the old fundamental sense. There were fewer who accepted the divine inspiration of the Bible or its literal truth. There were more who believed in progress or in economic law even when they continued to attend church or chapel on a Sunday. The only English census of church attendance was taken in 1851. It revealed that few of the industrial working class ever went to church or chapel.

The change was even more pronounced in political ideas. Despite the failure of the revolutions of 1848, liberalism triumphed everywhere to a greater or less degree. In 1871 Germany got unification and universal suffrage. Russia got a sort of constitution in 1906. Austria got universal suffrage in 1907. Even Turkey got a constitution in 1908, though it rarely operated. By the end of the period Monaco was the only European state with an absolute ruler. More fundamental was the decline in the political power of the landowning aristocracy, though not in their wealth. During the revolution of 1848 robot – the labour rent paid by the peasants for their holdings – was abolished throughout the Austrian Empire. Serfdom was abolished in Russia in 1861. Peasants were free to leave their holdings for the towns or for countries overseas. In time they began to organize their own peasant parties, as happened sensationally in Ireland. The town workers were more consciously aggressive. The Socialist parties that sprang up all over Europe were less significant for their doctrines than for their class consciousness. They were the parties of the industrial workers, as the title of the British Labour party showed at its clearest.

People were not only changing their ideas. There were also more people. The dynamic rise in population started in Great Britain during the eighteenth century. Now it began to operate all over Europe. Historians are not agreed as to why this happened. Some have pointed to improved medical services, though this is a doubtful factor in the more backward parts of Europe. Better sanitation may have counted, though it sometimes made things worse: water closets increased the incidence of typhoid as long as domestic sewers were allowed to contaminate the supply of drinking water. Some historians have prosaically remarked that people were eating more potatoes – a factor which carried the population of Ireland to the point of catastrophe. The immediate cause of the rise in population was probably a decline in infant mortality, but this itself is still in need of explanation. All we know is that population

10

Four little Swedish boys look out of their log cabin

was increasing at an unprecedented rate. When there was no corresponding increase in resources, famine followed – most notoriously in Ireland in 1846, but also in Spain and southern Italy later.

Throughout most of Europe the increase in food supplies took place. Even where aristocrats retained their great estates, they became agricultural businessmen, as much concerned to raise their rents or farm profits as to preserve their social position. The Hungarian nobility, for instance, continued to display their traditional dress and to pose as the descendants of Arpad and his companions. Nothing seemed more unchanging than life on the puszta, the great Hungarian plain. But in fact there were more steam ploughs in Hungary than in any other European country. Thanks to such innovations Europe could for a time still feed its growing populations. Later on food came more and more from overseas. The United States had a revolutionary effect on Europe in many ways. It offered a new home. It represented a democratic ideal. It also supplied wheat to the industrial countries of Europe, and England in particular. By 1914, ninety per cent of British wheat for bread was coming from overseas. The British farmer, when not ruined, preferred the more profitable, though more wasteful, activities of stock raising and dairy farming for the nearby towns.

Towns had existed in Europe since the early Middle Ages and played a more decisive part than their mere size indicated. They were the centres of finance, commerce and culture. Often they were the political capital which sometimes meant that they were also the residence of the monarch. The largest towns were rarely the centres of industry which, when they occurred at all, were usually found in the country near a good supply of water. Even the Industrial Revolution created new towns of medium size rather than adding to the great ones. In 1848 only London and Paris had more than a million inhabitants. By 1880 Berlin had joined them. By 1910 there were five more – Glasgow, Istanbul, Vienna, Moscow and St Petersburg. Only Glasgow and Moscow were not the political capitals, and Moscow had been and was to be again.

Nevertheless towns were the symbols of contemporary civilization as they had rarely been before. This was the age of the bourgeoisie, and bourgeois is merely the French word for a citizen – a town dweller. By 1851 more than half the English population was living in towns. Half a century later the Germans had joined them. Towns absorbed much of the increase in population. This development was aided by the new freedom of movement which in its turn had both political and physical causes. The new political freedom is often overlooked, perhaps because it is inconceivable to the present generation. We pride ourselves on our emancipation from the hindrances to movement which shackled previous generations. But it is now impossible to travel without a passport. In some countries visas – that is, permits to enter – are still required and these are often not given without securing a permit to work. In some countries it is impossible to leave without official permission.

All such restrictions were swept away during the second half of the nineteenth century. The change came with startling suddenness. Before 1848 a passport was required in the Austrian Empire even to go from one town to another, and the first people to disregard this regulation were the deputies elected to the Constituent Assembly at Vienna in the year of revolution. Within a few years all the barriers were down. Passports were abolished except for Russia and Turkey. No permits were needed to leave one country or go to another. By the mid-1870s most European currencies were based on gold and were freely interchangeable. A man living in London could decide at a moment's notice to settle in Vienna or Paris, and he could move himself and his possessions there the same day. Europeans had never enjoyed such freedom and were never to do so again.

This political freedom was of practical use only because of the physical freedom that went with it. Railways were the greatest stroke of emancipation in the history of mankind. Until the middle of the century men could move only as fast as their feet or a horse could carry them. The armies of Napoleon often won victories by their speed, but they went no faster than the Roman legions had done, and most armies went a good deal more slowly. Suddenly men who had moved at three or at best ten miles an hour could go at fifty, and that without any physical effort on their part. By 1848 only Great Britain and Belgium had established their main railway networks. British projectors and British workmen were beginning the creation of railways in France, much to the annoyance of Frenchmen with a vested interest in horse traffic. Fifty years later the European network was complete everywhere except in Russia, and there were more miles of railway than there are now. Geographic obstacles disappeared. The Semmering railway linked Vienna and Trieste in 1854, enabling Trieste to become a great port. The Mont Cenis tunnel through the Alps was opened in 1870, and other Alpine tunnels were soon to follow.

The rack-and-pinion Schafberg mountain railway in Austria

The railways brought unity to Europe despite the political divisions. Trains crossed the frontiers with little formality. The transcontinental expresses provided dining cars and sleeping cars, carrying passengers from one end of Europe to the other in conditions of unparallelled luxury. In 1888 the Oriental Express, most romantic of all trains, began to run from Calais and Paris to Istanbul. Man seemed to have conquered space. The railways terminus replaced the cathedral as the architectural achievement of the age. St Pancras station in London excelled in its Gothic fantasy. King's Cross, its immediate neighbour, was modelled on the Tsar's riding school at St Petersburg – an indication that railway passengers were now as important as monarchs.

Sea transport took longer to accept the reign of the steam engine. Until the 1860s the clippers were faster than steam-ships across the Atlantic. Sailing ships handled most of the world's carrying trade until the 1880s and even thereafter retained much of the local traffic. Fishing fleets in local waters still operated under sail, usually without an auxiliary engine. At the time of the Crimean War most of the Royal Navy was still composed of sailing ships, and until the first years of the twentieth century, British warships retained their masts and sails in case their engines broke down.

Nevertheless steam triumphed in the long run and nowhere more decisively than in the crossing of the Atlantic. This was the great field of the emigrant ship, carrying passengers at almost nominal rates and of course under inhuman conditions. Liverpool and Glasgow were the first emigrant ports. Soon they were joined by Hamburg and Bremen. The British were the first to move in large numbers, and the Germans followed. Later in the century the flood of emigrants came from Italy and eastern Europe with Russians last of all. A few emigrated for political reasons – Chartists from England, and German Radicals after the revolution of 1848. Most fled from hardship and starvation as the Irish did. Most of them believed they were going to the Promised Land. They were often disappointed.

The European continent was united in less tangible ways. The greatest achievement here was the electric telegraph which was invented in 1836–7. It was at first used in railway signalling. Soon it became general. There were 2,000 miles of telegraph lines in Europe in 1849, 111,000 twenty years later. England was linked to the continent by submarine cable in the early 1850s; Europe to America in 1865. Six years later cables girdled the globe. Here was an almost incredible advance in communications. From this moment men could

13

know what was happening in any part of the civilized world within a few minutes instead of after days or even months. By means of the electric cable, British troops returning from the Crimea were diverted to India at the time of the Mutiny. It was no accident that Julius Reuter founded his telegraph agency in 1851. News became world wide. So, too, did prices on the commodity markets of the world. Police and military administration relied on the telegraph. The private citizen was not forgotten. Most telegrams, it seems, were exchanged between relatives.

The improvements in communications brought with them international institutions. Telegrams prompted the International Telegraph Union of 1865. Railways carrying mail prompted the Universal Postal Union in 1875 with international coordination of postal rates, a Union that has continued to operate even between belligerent nations. Perhaps the most symbolic institution was the International Meteorological Organization of 1878. Previously countries had used their own meridian. French maps were drawn on the meridian of Paris, Dutch on that of Amsterdam. Now all accepted the meridian of Greenwich, though the Dutch were half-hearted about this until 1940 when they were forced into conformity by their German conquerors. It is a striking tribute to British astronomers and maritime supremacy that everyone in the world now sets his watch by Greenwich Mean Time, suitably adjusted plus or minus so many hours according to his geographical position.

Railways and steam ships not only promoted migration across the seas. They also promoted travel from one town to another. Provincial businessmen could go up to London or Vienna for the day. Families scattered over the country could visit each other instead of saying farewell for ever. Schoolboys could go home for the holidays instead of remaining at school for seven unbroken years as my great-grandfather did. Indeed railways produced that characteristic nineteenth-century invention, the holiday. Previously aristocrats and other rich people moved from their town to their country house for the summer, and fashionable people settled at Bath or Baden Baden for the winter. Most people never moved, though they sometimes took a day off. In the 1930s, I had an elderly neighbour in the Peak District who had been born in the house where he was still living and had never slept away from it for a single night. By then this was unusual. In earlier centuries it had been the common lot.

Now middle-class families went to the seaside or the

Holiday-makers in Deal, an English seaside resort, 1906

country for a fortnight's holiday in the summer. Brighton, which had previously been a resort of the fashionable, became the nearest playground for thousands of Londoners. Blackpool and Southport catered for industrial Lancashire. Dieppe took holiday makers from Paris. Leopold II equipped Ostend with palaces on the scale of Versailles from the profits of the Congo. The Riviera, discovered by Lord Brougham, provided for those rich enough to take a winter holiday as well as one in the summer.

The nineteenth century also discovered the countryside. Perhaps this came from reading Wordsworth's poetry. At any rate the Lake District, North Wales and the Scotch Highlands all had their holiday makers and their organized tours. River steamers took holiday makers up the Rhine. Switzerland had the greatest success. It became the play ground of Europe. Previously, though people had sometimes taken country walks, no one had thought of climbing mountains. Now this became a widespread enthusiasm among the middle classes. At the end of the century skis were introduced from Norway and improved for sporting purposes, thus making Switzerland as popular in the winter as it had been in the summer. Holidays as pleasure were in fact the most beneficent innovation of the nineteenth century.

There were still blank areas of the world waiting to be explored – Antarctica, nearly all Africa, much of Asia and some remote parts of Europe, especially in the Balkans. The explorer was a characteristic feature of the time, carrying with him mapping equipment, the Bible, gin and European firearms. As Belloc wrote in *The Modern Traveller*: 'We have got The Maxim gun and they have not'. By the end of the period nearly all the unknown world had been penetrated by European transport and ideas, though the Balkans did not become popular tourist resorts until after the second world war.

To our eyes there was one curious flaw in this story of easier movement. It was easy to move wherever there were railways or steamships. It was still difficult to make shorter journeys – from one village to the next, or even from one railway terminus to another in the great cities. France was the only country covered by a network of narrow-gauge railways, chugging along the country lanes or through the village streets. Everywhere else the horse still reigned for local movement. Visiting any city of the time, we should notice the general grime from steam trains and domestic coal fires. We should be struck even more by the smell of horse dung and the dirt in the streets. Crossing a street was a

daring venture, rarely attempted by a lady in a trailing skirt. The street sweeper was a figure as universal as the newspaper vendor.

The great age of the railway was thus paradoxically also the last great age of the horse. Though the stage coach and the diligence disappeared except in mountainous or backward districts, the horse still provided all local transport. Every big town house had its mews, and every country house its stables. Every great man and every fashionable doctor kept his own carriage. The nineteenth century, putting most things on a cash basis, also produced horse-drawn vehicles for hire, complete with taxi meters. England had its own speciality, the hansom cab, a two-wheeled vehicle with its driver perched at the back and sometimes called the gondola of the streets. Continental cities had four-wheelers: landaus, fiacres or, in honour of the great Queen, victorias. For humbler citizens there were horse-drawn omnibuses and sometimes horse-drawn trams.

Horses also did most of the agricultural work. Oxen drawing the plough could still be seen in Dorset in the 1880s, and a few can still be seen in eastern Europe. At the other end of the scale, the steam plough was an occasional rival to the horse. But the usual rural scene was the ploughman and his horse turning the furrows. The farmer, the country doctor and the country clergyman did their rounds on horseback, though the continental priest was probably too poor to afford one. Fox hunting on horseback flourished in England and Ireland and was imitated by continental aristocrats in France and Hungary who prided themselves, rightly or wrongly, on their resemblance to English milords.

A great improvement in city transport came in 1889 when Siemans, a German engineer, invented the electric tram. Soon every city in Europe, indeed every city in the world, had its trams. London had its trams. Manchester had its trams. Paris had its trams. So did Moscow, Palermo and even Istanbul. The tram was the first civic blow at the dominance of the horse. London, usually a centre of initiative, was curiously backward. The House of Lords would not allow trams along the Embankment or across the Thames bridges. Hence the City and the West End had to rely on horse-drawn omnibuses until the first decade of the twentieth century. English cities were also the only ones with two-decker trams, perhaps on the omnibus model.

The dominance of the horse was further shaken by the coming of the bicycle. For the first time travellers were not tied to the iron rail. In its early days the bicycle, still rather

Traffic in the Strand, London
in the 1890s

an uncomfortable vehicle, was quite a fashionable form of travel. Aristocrats going off for the weekend took their bicycles with them and rode on them from the local station to their country house. H. G. Wells dedicated a whole novel to them, revealingly called *The Wheels of Chance*. The final blow to both horse and railway was at any rate foreshadowed before the outbreak of the first world war. This was the internal combustion engine and its instrument, the automobile or motor car. At first this was used mainly for public transport. The huge private cars or horseless carriages remained a luxury until after the first world war. Rich people went for drives or occasionally for tours. Jack Tanner in Shaw's play *Man and Superman* set out to drive from England to Morocco, though he was trapped by a designing female, Ann Whitefield, in the Spanish Sierra.

Electricity was a great civilizer in other ways. It began to replace gas for street lighting, and the city streets became well lit for the first time. This no doubt helped to reduce the violence which till then had been common. Garrotting had been a more painful form of mugging in the 1860s. Policemen patrolled the poorer quarters of cities in pairs, and there were many city streets where they did not dare to venture at all. Women of the more respectable classes never went out unattended. The violence was not all on one side. Public executions continued in England until the 1860s and in France until the twentieth century.

Recreation was another civilizing force. There had always of course been popular sports – rough games, combats with single stick, cock fighting and bear baiting. Now the crueller sports were made illegal, though this did not always end them. Games with codes of rules flourished, some to play and some to watch. Association football was England's great gift to the world, one that will survive when all other English achievements are forgotten. Lawn tennis, another invention of the elegant English upper classes, also became universal later, and the Scotch made their own contribution with their national game, golf.

The great cities of Europe reached new pinnacles of glory. Resplendent town halls rivalled the railway stations and symbolized bourgeois civilization at its highest. On the continent they usually followed the Gothic models of the mediaeval Hotel de Ville or Rathaus, as in Paris and Vienna. English towns, more eclectic, varied between Gothic and Classical, in either case palatial. Every continental city had its great opera house, another symbol of bourgeois triumph. Previously opera had been the entertainment of princely courts. Now bourgeois audiences were accommodated as well. Even London had its opera house at Covent Garden, though no regular opera company. And even Edward VII dragged himself to the annual cycles of Wagner's Ring, though he ate and drank during much of the performance.

A London backstreet in 1892

Continental cities also developed cafés, social centres often of great magnificence. Of course there had been coffee houses for a long time, and the original cafés still flourished in eastern Europe – primitive buildings where the customers sat cross-legged, smoking hookah pipes. The new cafés were different – vast halls glittering with mirrors, each one with its special clientele. Some were for artists, some for politicians, some for writers and some for chess players. Here again England was an exception. There were few great cafés, only the Café Royal, an importation from France as its name and the N (for Napoleon III) on its façade implied. The English social centre was the club, also palatial, and each also with its special membership. There were Reform clubs for the Liberals and Carlton Clubs for the Conservatives, Athenaeum Clubs for aspiring intellectuals and Crockfords for card players. There were a few continental imitations such as the Jockey Club in Paris. Essentially the club was an English institution.

There was another side to city life. A mile or so away from the grandiose centres people were living in worse conditions than those that they had fled from in their peasant homes. The slum was as universal as the town hall or opera house. The swarm of new arrivals was relegated to decaying houses and worked in sweat shops for starvation wages. Every big city – London, Paris, Vienna and Berlin – had its slum area, breeding disease which often spread to the bourgeois quarters. Poverty in the countryside had its redeeming features. In the cities it had none. Photographs of slum dwellers and especially of slum children are a reminder that this age of bourgeois civilization brought greater prosperity and wealth for a few and greater hardships for the many.

The contrasts between the rich and the poor, between those who had moved with the times and those who had stood still, were greater and more savage than before. Until the nineteenth century even the wealthiest classes, even kings and queens, lived in conditions that we should now find appalling: no sanitation, no pure water, no efficient medical services, hideous discomfort when travelling. Now a few had escaped from these hardships. The rest were still exploited and still suffered. The cleavage was purely of class and historical tradition, not innate. All Europeans were of the

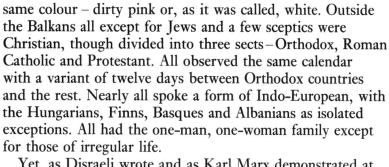

same colour – dirty pink or, as it was called, white. Outside the Balkans all except for Jews and a few sceptics were Christian, though divided into three sects – Orthodox, Roman Catholic and Protestant. All observed the same calendar with a variant of twelve days between Orthodox countries and the rest. Nearly all spoke a form of Indo-European, with the Hungarians, Finns, Basques and Albanians as isolated exceptions. All had the one-man, one-woman family except for those of irregular life.

Yet, as Disraeli wrote and as Karl Marx demonstrated at length, there were Two Nations, which seemed to differ as much as black and white. The cleavage took on many aspects. Despite the industrial boom, only Germany and Great Britain were fully advanced communities where industry predominated. There was a middle zone of France, Italy and Austria-Hungary, where industry and agriculture still balanced. Eastern Europe was barely touched by the new civilization except for the intruding railways. There life went on unchanged as it had done since time immemorial. Centuries seemed to divide the Ringstrasse in Vienna from the Balkan peasant village. Yet they were only a day's train journey away from each other.

The cleavage was not merely geographic. It existed within each country. English agricultural labourers still wore smocks. Peasants everywhere clung to traditional costume not for display but because it was the only possession they had. Such costumes could be seen as much in Dutch villages as in Albania or wildest Spain. If by the typical European we mean the majority of Europeans, then the typical European still lived on the edge of starvation and still worked unlimited hours for inadequate reward. He was illiterate, his mind a jumble of superstition and rural cunning. He never left his village, knew nothing of politics and accepted unquestioningly the religion he was taught by the priest.

One factor pulled town and country, rich and poor, new and old together. Though the industrial system created great things, it had less effect on small ones. The craftsman still held his own. Factories produced cotton or wool cloth. But the shirts, dresses or suits made from them were produced by hand. The village tailor cross-legged with his needle was no different from the smart tailor in Bond Street, except that he received less for his work. Poor people made their clothes at home or adapted the cast-offs of the rich. Shoes were made by hand, and the village cobbler was the local Radical in England, though not in the Balkans. Much of the furniture in poorer homes was made by craftsmen and handed down from generation to generation. The survival of the horse demanded a smithy in every village. The horse's harness was the work of craftsmen. Great breweries relied on craftsmen to make the beer barrels. Craftsmen and industrial workers were worlds apart even if they appeared under the same heading in the census returns.

Retail selling was another occupation almost untouched by the new spirit. Many commodities were already traded on a world market, yet when these same commodities finally reached the consumer, this was in a small shop handling only a few goods and probably run by the proprietor and his family. The shopkeeper was a survival from a pre-industrial age of individual trading on a small scale. He was the essential 'little man', sometimes a Radical in politics but sometimes enthusiastic for a plebiscitarian dictator such as Napoleon III or, in later days, Hitler. There were street markets in every town and the great fairs still flourished alongside the new international markets of London. There were already a few multiple stores such as Printemps in Paris and Harrods in London. But the village shopkeeper handled more goods everywhere from Great Britain to the Balkans.

The greatest unifying force was also paradoxically the greatest cause of division. This was nationalism, the dominating political feature of the nineteenth century. Previously men had often felt patriotic loyalty towards an existing state. Now they developed national consciousness and national pride. The national idea was a creation of the French revolution, carried across Europe by the revolutions of 1848. But the greatest missionary of nationalism was the school teacher. An illiterate man does not know what nation he belongs to. He can only say, 'I come from here'. Once he can read and write, he uses the national language and soon knows he is doing so. Universal primary education was established in most European countries during the later nineteenth century. The village school became almost as common as the village church, usually cooperating with it, sometimes, especially in France, promoting a rival creed. The education provided was often crude and in eastern Europe far from universal. Nevertheless the decline in illiteracy was as striking as the increase in population.

Higher education also served the cause of nationalism, extolling national traditions as well as spreading the national language. Historians especially were exponents of the national cause. They wrote national histories designed to emphasize the peculiar greatness of their particular nation. German historians played a leading part in the creation of German

A tunny fish market in Palermo, Sicily

unity. English historians exalted the British constitution and the British Empire. French historians paraded the achievements of the great revolution and the glory of Napoleon. On a more popular level daily newspapers helped to strengthen national unity. They were a recent invention, symbolizing the triumph of the machine, in their case the steam press. Railways enabled them to cover the country where previously they had been local. By the end of the century Englishmen were reading much the same news each morning. Public opinion in the modern sense had been born.

Education weakened local speech and local loyalties. Sir Robert Peel was the last English Prime Minister with a local accent (Lancashire), though there were of course Prime Ministers with a Welsh or Scotch accent in the twentieth century. Frenchmen thought of themselves as French, not as Normans or Provencals. All Germans could speak *hoch Deutsch* (High German) though they retained their provincial speech for family use. Italy is perhaps the most impressive case. Italy had never been a political unit. Speech differed so much from state to state as almost to be different languages. Few Neapolitans felt that they had anything in common with Venetians or Piedmontese. Yet within a comparatively few years Italian nationalism swept all before it. Italy became a rigorously unified state, and all Italians spoke Tuscan.

The most practical and perhaps the most powerful expression of nationalism was the army or as it was often called 'the nation in arms'. The old armies had been composed of long-term conscripts, isolated from the rest of the community. The victories of the short-service Prussian army in 1866 and 1870 caused a general conversion. All continental countries went over to universal military service for a two- or three-year period. The soldier came from the civilian community, and nearly all males in that community had been soldiers. During their period of service the soldiers wore 'uniform', its very name implying the ironing out of local differences. The process was of course never complete. Crack cavalry regiments such as the German Death's Head Hussars, wore exotic uniforms that were survivals from a more barbaric age, and in most armies class differences prevented any uniformity between officers and other ranks. Great Britain was a clear exception to the continental pattern, clinging to a professional army and navy until the first world war. Even so, countless music hall songs and Kipling's poetry bear witness that the British army and the Royal Navy had also become symbols of national pride.

In the early days of nationalism men assumed that it would

21

reinforce the existing great states or create new ones. Great Britain and France would be even greater; a united Germany and a new Italy would join them. Lesser nationalities, when considered at all, were dismissed as picturesque survivals of the same kind as spinning wheels or peasant costume and like them doomed to disappear in the modern industrial age. This view was particularly common among men of radical opinion, impatient with the past. Marx and Engels for instance expected that such 'tribes' as the Czechs or the Croats would simply be eaten up by the German nation. At first this seemed likely to happen. Very few Frenchmen worried in the nineteenth century about the Breton or the Basque problem. Very few Englishmen worried about the Welsh problem and most Englishmen assumed that the Scotch were delighted to have become next door to English people. The English certainly worried about the Irish problem but much more on religious and economic than on national grounds, at any rate until the end of the century. Even so the English had one unique victory. At the beginning of the nineteenth century nearly all native Irishmen spoke their national tongue, Erse. At the end of the nineteenth century, thanks to an intensive system of English education, virtually none did so. There is no other case in Europe of the disappearance of a national language, at any rate since the death of Cornish in the seventeenth century. It was however far from meaning the disappearance of the Irish nation.

National survivals or revivals struck deeper in eastern Europe. The prophecy of Marx and Engels was not fulfilled. Half-forgotten nations became fully conscious and were joined by nations such as the Slovaks who had been forgotten altogether. The Austrian Empire, or Austria-Hungary as it was called after 1867, was the one Great Power that failed to transform itself into a national state, though Hungary claimed to have done so. The Czechs had their own opera house and their own musical composers such as Dvorak and Smetana who, though assertively national, were clearly of European stature. They had their own university as did also the Croats and the Serbs. The Ottoman Empire was in even worse case. Its military rule over Christian Balkan peoples, could never take on a Turkish national character. Instead the series of wars culminating in the Balkan wars of 1912–13 were wars of national liberation.

War in general provided a curious contradiction throughout this period. Many observers believed that Europe had become too civilized to resort to war or, to put it another way, that

Kaiser William II and King George V, 1913

peace – in this case the advance of industry – had its victories no less renowned than war. Nevertheless the first twenty years of the period, between 1850 and 1870, saw a series of wars: the first, the Crimean war, a confused muddle, and the others wars of national purpose if not of liberation. In 1859 the French and Sardinians ended Austrian predominance in Italy, a process completed in 1866. In 1864 Austria and Prussia acquired Sleswig and Holstein from Denmark in the name of German nationalism. Finally Prussia united Germany, or most of it, by defeating Austria in 1866 and France in 1870. Thereafter to everyone's surprise there were no more serious wars in Europe for more than a generation except for the Balkan war between Russia and Turkey in 1877–8. Instead there was the Armed Peace with every Great Power increasing its military forces, Austria-Hungary and Italy somewhat ineffectually.

In some ways these forces were modern. Railways for instance played a decisive part in Prussia's victories. All plans for mobilization centred on the railways, and generals had to be expert in railway time tables. The new steel industry supplied the guns for the armies and the material for the battleships. In other ways the military forces remained stuck in the past. The horse was still their only means of transport, with forage for the horses providing as great a problem as food and munitions for the men. Tactics on the battlefield were unchanged from the days of Napoleon: masses of men flung against each other in ever greater number. Uniforms were still gaudy until the British developed khaki during the Anglo-Boer war. No general ever consulted a scientist or an industrial leader. For them the Industrial Revolution had not taken place.

The Armed Peace had great political effects. The military forces and virtues were still exalted. Monarchs found a new occupation in symbolizing the nation in arms just when their political functions were diminishing. Some monarchs still chose their ministers. Few determined policy. But they concealed this by parading their military character. European monarchs on their public appearances always wore military uniform, dressing up as Field Marshals, Honorary Colonels or Admirals of the Fleet. This was new. In earlier ages monarchs did not wear military uniform unless they were actually serving officers. Louis XIV did not do so. Nor did George IV, earlier the Prince Regent, despite his claim to have been present at the battle of Waterloo. The practice was commoner among the German princes and perhaps became universal in the later nineteenth century because nearly all monarchs after the fall of Napoleon III were either Germans, of German descent or married to Germans. Every English sovereign for instance between Queen Anne and George V had a German mother, except of course for Edward VII who had a German father.

The European monarchs had a field day in this period thanks to the railways. They could move about more freely and took advantage of this to meet each other constantly, showing themselves off to their peoples on the way. Germany was their favourite meeting place, partly because of its central position and partly because of the family connections most monarchs had there. The Tsar went there nearly every year. Edward VII passed through Germany and called on his German relatives on his way to Marienbad. France, having become the only republic in Europe in 1871, missed most of these royal visitors except for the unofficial visits of Edward VII to Paris when Prince of Wales. But Russian Grand Dukes settled on the Riviera with their ballerina mistresses, and Queen Victoria, travelling as the Duchess of Lancaster, often went there in her old age.

The monarchs were often called 'the crowned heads of Europe'. Few of them however actually held a coronation. The smart new ceremony took the form of an oath to the constitution. Franz Joseph managed to be crowned King of Hungary in 1867, but there was no coronation for the recently invented Emperor of Austria. Nor was there any coronation ceremony for the German Emperor. In England, George IV's was the last full-blown coronation. William IV had a cut-price one, and the example was followed by his successors. Victoria atoned for this by celebrating both her golden and her diamond jubilees. Only the Tsars maintained the ancient splendour, and the coronation of Nicholas II was a last blaze of the old Europe, recalling the great days of Byzantium.

Monarchs were symbols of social stability as well as of nationalism. The social peril was still supposed to be great. The one great outbreak of political violence was the Paris Commune of 1871, which was not so much a proletarian or socialist revolution, despite Marx's championing of it, as a spontaneous protest by the Paris poor against defeat and harsh conditions. The Commune was suppressed with great savagery – twenty thousand or more were killed, over ten thousand transported. This was a curious commentary on the claim of the bourgeoisie to be more civilized and tolerant than the absolute monarchs. Despite this most Socialist parties, even when theoretically Marxist, lost their

Winston Churchill at the battle
of Sydney Street in East
London, 1911

revolutionary character and came to believe that the social
revolution would be achieved automatically once they had
won a majority of votes. The ballot box superseded the
barricades.

There were still exiled revolutionaries, now mostly Russian
where they had previously been French or Italian. Anarchists
were a speciality of the period. They commanded a sizeable
following in Italy and Spain. Otherwise they were lone
operators, hoping to provoke a social collapse by individual
acts of violence, like Conrad's Secret Agent who, however,
only caused an explosion by accident. Monarchs were the
favourite target of the anarchists and of their Russian
counterpart the nihilists. The anarchist bag was considerable:
a Tsar of Russia, a King of Italy, an Austrian Empress and a
French President.

There were also immigrants to western Europe of a
different political kind. These were the Russian Jews, fleeing
from the pogroms and lesser brutalities that tsarist
governments sought to maintain themselves by. Vienna and
Berlin had their Jewish quarters. In London the Jews took
over much of the East End from the earlier slum-dwellers.
Russian anti-semitism was of the traditional kind that was
as old as Christianity itself. There was also a new political
anti-semitism, partly a bastard product of nationalism and
partly a product of economic jealousy. There were
anti-semitic political parties in Austria and Germany. In
France anti-semitism provoked in the Dreyfus case the
gravest crisis of the Third Republic. Anti-Jewish riots were

not uncommon in English towns and quite common in Welsh ones. Curiously, while poor Jews usually settled in London or Leeds when they could not move on to America, Jewish intellectuals preferred central Europe – Berlin or Vienna – and Germany was generally regarded as giving Jews the warmest welcome. Even in the first world war the British government took up Zionism in order to win over European and American Jews who it was believed would otherwise support Germany.

Balkan peasants on their way home from cattle market
Below: London suffragettes demonstrate, 1910

We know a great deal about the later nineteenth century. There are far more statistics than for any previous age. Indeed reliance on fairly accurate statistics became common for both political and economic purposes. There are far more records ranging from newspapers to the papers of government departments. There are reports of parliamentary debates, many of them verbatim. There was more serious study of economic and political problems. There were more observers of other countries, studying everything from folk lore to contemporary art. Yet virtually all the books and articles written then and most of those written since by historians leave out half the human race. It would almost seem that European men appeared in the world fully grown or were brought into it by the agency of storks. In fact at least half the inhabitants of Europe and probably a little more were women. Neglect of them was evidently a characteristic of the age, and continuance of this neglect indicates that most writers, especially historians, have not outgrown nineteenth-century habits.

Surely women too did not pass through this age of change unaffected. The legal changes are easiest to identify. In many countries there were restrictions on the work women could do in industries and limits on the hours they could work. Mining was often forbidden to them altogether. Women had always taught in the lowest level of primary schools, and now other professions were grudgingly opened to them, beginning with medicine. A few were able to attend universities. There were a few women journalists and even daring women explorers of Asia and Africa. Women gifted enough to become writers, especially novelists, could escape from their inferior position almost completely. No one could suppose that George Sand was unemancipated, and many, including Gladstone, read the works of Mrs Humphrey Ward as though they were a new gospel.

For the great majority of women life was what it had always been: domestic service for either their husbands or for an employer. No man in any class ever did any domestic

work of any kind. In Ireland or the Balkans where man, wife and donkey went together to market, the man returned home on the donkey and the wife trudged behind carrying the day's purchases. Even in Great Britain, the most industrialized country, domestic service was still the largest single occupation. Indeed the later nineteenth century was the golden age for the employer of domestic servants. In the seventeenth century Pepys, a top civil servant at the admiralty, had one resident female servant. His nineteenth-century successor had six. Higher up the social scale noblemen had households of fifty or more. The Earl of Derby for instance had one dining hall for his guests, a second for the fifty upper servants, and a gloomy dungeon for the lowest rank of servants who did all the menial work and waited on the upper servants. A Hungarian count often had a town palace and three or four in the country, each with a staff of eighty.

In well-to-do houses there was usually a housekeeper as intermediary between her employer and the maid servants. In great houses there were separate staircases for the domestic servants who lived in tiny cells under the roof, often with forty of them sharing one cold-water tap. Domestic service was drudgery unaided by modern ingenuity. Coal had to be carried by hand often to the bedrooms as well as to the living rooms. The daily bath, now usual with the upper classes, meant that hot water had to be carried to every bedroom and then carried away. Coal fires involved the daily dusting of rooms, a particularly laborious task thanks to the clutter of bric-à-brac. The domestic servant was a 'slavey', her position redeemed only by the sense of belonging, in however degraded a way, to a community.

In all the welter of modern inventions few benefited women. One was the sewing machine, developed during the 1850s. Often it was the only machine women ever saw, certainly the only one they ever used. In domestic use it was an unmixed blessing. In wider use it added to women's burdens. The song of the shirt was now the song of the sewing machine. In the sweat shops of the city slums women, working sewing machines, were driven harder than before, and their sufferings were one of the scandals of the age.

Perhaps the typewriter should be added to women's blessings, at any rate towards the end of the period. In time it enabled the woman typist to replace the male clerk with his elegant copy hand. But most of this happened only during and after the first world war. The bicycle was a true emancipator. Women as much as men used it from the first and thus acquired a new freedom of movement. The bicycle also helped to stimulate the first step towards more rational women's clothing, in this case bloomers. But the pictures of this period show that women, particularly in the upper classes, took little advantage of their emancipation. Even the suffragettes were attired in the height of fashion, with hobble skirts and picture hats.

The greatest step towards women's emancipation is also the one most difficult to explain or even to document. During the later nineteenth century the birth rate began to decline in most European countries, most markedly in the most advanced. Women were bearing fewer children. We do not know why or how. Was there some rational choice in favour of fewer children? If so, how did it spread across Europe, in villages as much as in towns, in Roman Catholic countries as much as in Protestant ones? Were there more abortions? Were artificial means of birth control used, presumably the sheath? There was a certain amount of illicit contraceptive propaganda, but surely too little to produce such decisive effects. One gets the impression of a vast secret society of women spreading the glad tidings in ways that no historian will ever detect. At any rate it happened. Women were bearing fewer children, one of the greatest revolutions in the story of mankind.

In other ways women were far from emancipation sexually. The principle of one sexual law for men and another for women reached its highest point in the later nineteenth century. Gladstone said that he had known eleven British Prime Ministers and that seven of them had been adulterers. The twentieth-century figure is much lower. Respectable married women were supposed to have no sexual feelings though plenty of children. As Lord Curzon said, 'Ladies don't move'. Women lower down the social scale were regarded as providing the safety valve for rigid morality higher up. There were probably more prostitutes than ever before though there is no precise means of knowing how many. Every continental town had its brothel which often acted also as social centre and café. In the capitalist order of the day women, too, became a commodity to be freely bought and sold. On the other hand protests against this double system were beginning to grow. The demand for the equality of women did not have to wait for the twentieth century.

Wherever we look there is the same clash between what had been and what was to come. On the whole the principles of change and movement were still winning. Despite all the

A boy soldier, 1914

differences of class, region, occupation and even sex, Europeans were becoming more alike. Trade-union leaders in their group photographs look indistinguishable from employers: the same clothes, the same beards, the same gold watch-chains across their portly stomachs. Girls on the beach at Brighton in the early twentieth century were wearing dresses not all that different from those worn at Ascot. Third-class railway carriages had become not much less comfortable, though sometimes more crowded, than first class. A Bulgarian Prime Minister looked much like a British Prime Minister, pursued much the same policies and used much the same political phrases in his speeches. Socialists came together in the Second International and even interfered in each other's domestic affairs, forbidding French Socialists for instance to become members of bourgeois governments.

State frontiers seemed to have lost most of their significance. Men crossed them freely and so did ideas. There has never been a time when European culture was so truly one. Tolstoy was the most highly regarded novelist in every European country. Shaw's plays were more widely performed in Germany than in England, and Germans spoke of 'unser Shakespeare' without provoking a smile. Stravinsky's *Rite of Spring* provoked a riot when it was performed in Paris, not however on nationalist grounds. The Hallé orchestra in Manchester had a German conductor. English artists settled in Étretat, and artists from every country found their home in Paris. Nearly everywhere men could be sure of reasonably fair treatment in courts of law. No one except the Russian Jews was killed for religious reasons. No one was killed for political reasons despite the synthetic outbursts of political rhetoric. There was security at all levels. Men and even women could walk the streets safe from violence and as yet pretty safe from the automobile. Money was safe from fluctuations. Even the poor were becoming less insecure and were protected from the extreme rigours of poverty and unemployment. The wonders of science were spread wide before mankind. It was a golden age or seems so in retrospect.

For this miraculous age of prosperity and security ended abruptly in 1914 with the outbreak of the greatest war ever known. In June 1914 Europe was in a state of profound peace as it had been for forty years past. A month later all the Great Powers of Europe except Italy were at war, and Italy joined in nine months later. Old Europe perished, and much of new Europe perished also. New differences arose, and Europe was not to know unity again.

THE EYE
OF THE CAMERA

A new visual record of history in the making

Above: Six photographs from a sequence showing a horse jumping a hurdle. These pictures were taken by Ottomar Anschütz in 1886 for the Military Riding Institute, Hanover. Opposite below: Calotype of 1844 of William Fox Talbot's photographic establishment at Reading.
Below: Photograph taken in Germany in 1887, the first to show the recoil of a gun

UP FOR THE
CORONATION

A tour of the Moscow streets 1896

Opposite: St Basil's Cathedral. Above and below left: Decorated streets. Below right: Tsar's bell in the Kremlin

Above: Children in a railway carriage
Below: The interior of the Cathedral
of the Saviour built to celebrate the
victory over Napoleon (now
demolished)

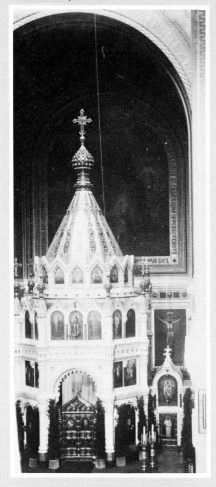

Above: A street vendor. Below: A *Droshki* in Moscow park.
Opposite: A toy shop

Opposite: The Red Gate. Above: A water-carrier
Below: Collectors for religious charities, and a peasant woman and child

DYNASTIC SPLENDOUR

Spectacular twilight of Europe's monarchies

Left: The Emperor Napoleon III of France with the Empress Eugénie and their only son the Prince Imperial, in 1860
Below: King Nicholas and Queen Milena of Montenegro with their family. Behind them, on the right, stand their three sons, Crown Prince Danilo, Prince Mirko and Prince Peter

A family photograph taken by the Danish King outside the Russian pavilion in Fredensborg Castle
Below: King Victor Emmanuel III of Italy with family (inset) and opening the Turin Exhibition

King Alfonso of Spain with his Queen, 'Ena', granddaughter of Queen Victoria, and their first son, the Prince of the Asturias

Left: Tsar Nicholas II wearing the Russian imperial costume of Tsar Alexis Michailovitch (1645–76) for the 'Boyar ball', 1903
Below: The Russian and Roumanian royal families. Queen Elizabeth of Roumania is seated to the right of the Tsar, with King Carol behind her
Opposite above: Tsar Nicholas II with the Tsarina 'Alix' and their family aboard the royal yacht 'Standart'

Opposite below: The Dowager Empress photographed at a festival in St. Petersburg with her son, Tsar Nicholas II (left), and the Tsarina (right)

The bust of the deceased Prince Albert dominates this wedding group photographed in March 1863, one hour after the marriage of Albert Edward, Prince of Wales, and Princess Alexandra of Denmark

Four generations of British monarchy: Queen Victoria with three future kings—Edward VII, George V and Edward VIII. Below: London's Regent Street celebrates Queen Victoria's Diamond Jubilee, 1897

A souvenir of the *entente cordiale* of 1903, showing Edward VII with President Fallières of France

Below: Royal splendour: Albert Edward, Prince of Wales, with two of his brothers

The Austrian royal family in 1859. The Emperor
Franz Josef is shown on the left, next to his brother
Maximilian (later Emperor of Mexico). Franz Josef's
Empress Elizabeth is sitting on the couch holding
Crown Prince Rudolf
Right: The Emperor Franz Josef with his young son
Prince Rudolf at Ischl in Austria

Victoria Louise, Duchess of Brunswick, wearing the uniform of the Danzig Death's Head Hussars
Left: Prince William of Prussia (later the Kaiser William II) with Crown Prince Rudolf of Austria-Hungary (right)

Prince Leopold of Bavaria at leisure. Above:
Preparing to go shooting. Opposite above: On a
sledging expedition in the Tyrol. Right: Surrounded
by his family (the Prince is seated second from the
right)

WORKSHOP OF THE WORLD

Industry and commerce

Left: An International Exhibition at the Crystal Palace
Below: Cotton mills in Lancashire

The International Paris Exhibition of 1889. Below:
The *Salle des Fêtes* of the Trocadero Palace, built
specially for the Exhibition. Bottom: Crowds of
exhibition visitors on the second stage of the newly-
constructed Eiffel Tower. Right: Great machinery
pavilion

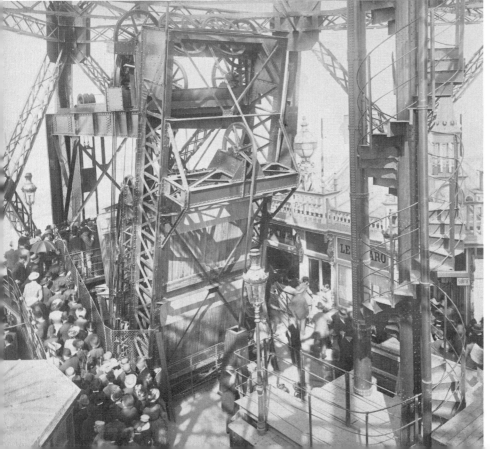

The oil fields of Roumania. Inset: View of the Moreni Pascov field in the Prahova valley. Below: An oil derrick collapsing after an explosion

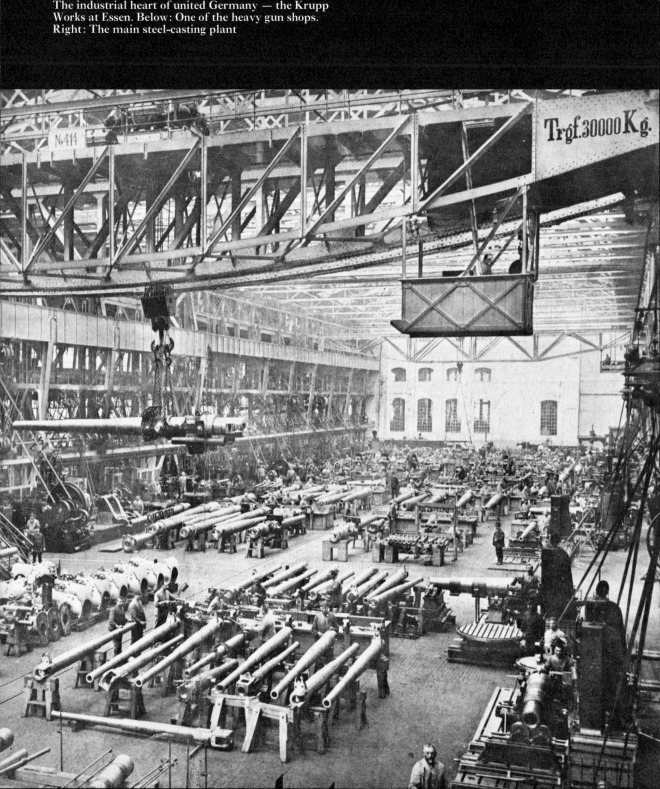

The industrial heart of united Germany — the Krupp
Works at Essen. Below: One of the heavy gun shops.
Right: The main steel-casting plant

Above and right: A clothes shop in Reykjavik in Iceland

Below: Harrods, London's fashionable store, Brompton Road, 1905

Haymakers at work in Norway

RURAL CONTRASTS

The face of the countryside

Scenes from the English countryside. Opposite above: Blacksmiths outside their forge at Alderley in 1896. Opposite below: Hedging in Lincolnshire in 1880

Ireland at the turn of the century. Below: A milkman on his rounds. Bottom: A peasant cottage in Glen Columbkille in Co. Donegal

Rural France. Oxen pulling a haycart at Aix-les-Bains   Below: Shepherds on stilts in the Landes district

Harvesting grapes at a vineyard in Burgundy

Above: Farmers of the Landes district of south-west France attending market

Below: A peasant family in the Minho Valley, north Portugal

Opposite above: Foresters of St Gall, Switzerland, eating their lunch
Opposite below: An alpenhorn blower of Grindelwald, Switzerland

Scenes from the Italian countryside. A peasant's home on the Via Appia. Inset: Oxen drawing a wine cart, from Bologna

Right: Slovak shepherd
Opposite: Turkish peasants
Below: Cattle at a well on the
Hortobagy Puszta, Hungary

Festivities in Bulgaria. Women dancing at a peasant wedding

Performing bears on the road in Turkey

TWO NATIONS
Rich and poor

Opposite above: The English wealthy at leisure:
croquet and hammocks, *c.* 1870
Above: A monument to Victorian opulence:
WS Gilbert's Grim's Dyke in Bushey, Middlesex
Left: A prosperous middle-class family group. This
photograph was taken in Istanbul, but could have
been of a family of similar social level from any part
of Europe

75

Rural poverty in Poland. Below: A *moujik* family on the steps of their cottage. Bottom: The interior of a peasant's hut

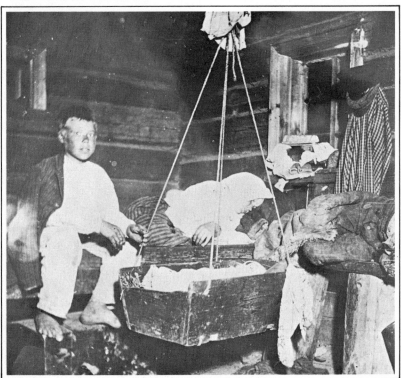

Slum yard in Kensington, London

THE GHETTO

'Huddled masses yearning to breathe free'

Left: A destitute Jew in Warsaw
Right: Jewish street tramps in the fruit market in Warsaw
Far right: The synagogue and town hall in the ghetto, Prague
Below: Jewish children at the ghetto pump, Cracow

RELIGION
Variety of observance and ritual

Opposite: Church service in Zeeland, Holland. Above: Peasants in Alsace returning from mass

Norwegian peasants in Sunday costume,
photographed in front of their church

Below: Swiss mummers in medieval costume,
celebrating the feast of St Nicholas at St Gall
Bottom: Belgian boys in church

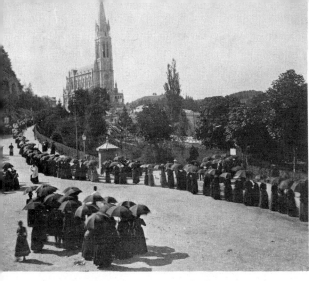

Opposite: The Italian brotherhood of Misericordia.
Above: Brothers carrying a sick man to their hospital
in Rome
Below: A member of the order in Florence

Left: Pilgrims queue to visit the miraculous grotto at
Lourdes
Below: Easter celebrations in Spain: the annual
procession leaving the Ermita de Jesus at Murcia

Nineteenth-century Bulgaria embraced two religions.
Above: Mohammedans praying before their mosque.
Below: A Greek Orthodox priest leads his flock in a
peasant funeral

A Mohammedan in Serbia, carrying home a ram for the celebration of Beiram

Sunday service in a village church in Transylvania. The two sexes are separated, and the unmarried women wear hats

Two religious ceremonies in nineteenth-century
Russia. Left: The Easter ceremony of 'raising the
dead who are alive'. A paralytic is carried forward to
be blessed by the priest and to kiss an ikon which is
said to have miraculous curative powers.
Below: A procession on the way to the Neva for the
ceremony of baptizing the river

Whirling dervishes in Konya, Anatolian Turkey.
Below: A group of dervishes reading the Koran.
Bottom: Dervishes preparing to whirl

Opposite: The interior of a Turkish mosque at
Broussa
Overleaf: A Moslem cemetery in Istanbul

London at the turn of the century. Below: Children
dancing to a street organ. Opposite: Rush hour on
one of the City bridges

URBAN LIFE

Street scenes and great cities in their heyday

Horse traffic becoming entangled at the junction of
Princes Street and Threadneedle Street, near the
Bank of England

Above: Nyhavn, the dockside area of Copenhagen, once the home of Hans Christian Andersen

Below left: A street scene in Reykjavik in Iceland. Below: The Bourse and Boulevard Anspach, Brussels

Canal scene in nineteenth-century Amsterdam

A goatherd with his flock in a suburb of Paris

Place Massena in Nice, just before the first world war

Street life in Naples. Below: The harbour. Left: A fish
stall in the Basso Porto. Bottom: A melon seller

street scene in Graz, Austria

Opposite above: A general view of Cologne with the
River Rhine and the Bridge of Boats
Opposite below: The Marienplatz in Munich

Opposite: The fish market in Danzig
Below: Zamkovy Square in Warsaw. On the right is
the old palace of the kings of Poland

General view of Tiflis, the capital of Georgia. Inset: A street scene in Tiflis

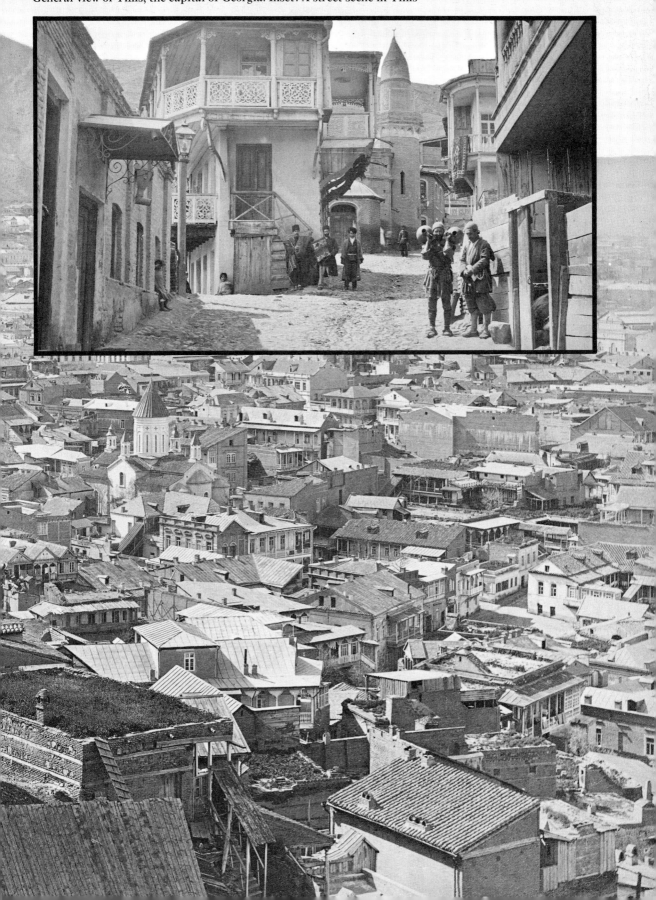

116

Street scenes in Istanbul. Far left: A rag-picker. Left: The melon market. Below: The boot market

The St Petersburg fire brigade. Right: Ringing the
alarm bell. The chart underneath the clock shows the
code of fire signals which were raised on the tower of
the fire station to indicate the location of the fire. Far
right: Members of the fire brigade with their fire
engine.
Below: A general view of Moscow with the Kremlin
and the royal palace

THE NEW TRANSPORT

Trains and cars

London Bridge Station at the turn of the century with horse-drawn mail vans

Two of London's principal stations. Opposite above: Victoria, terminus of the South Eastern & Chatham Railway in 1901 or 1902. Opposite below: Waterloo, terminus of the London & South Western Railway, at the turn of the century

Below: Ventnor Station on the Isle of Wight, c. 1880
Bottom: Commuter train about to depart from a London station, 1885

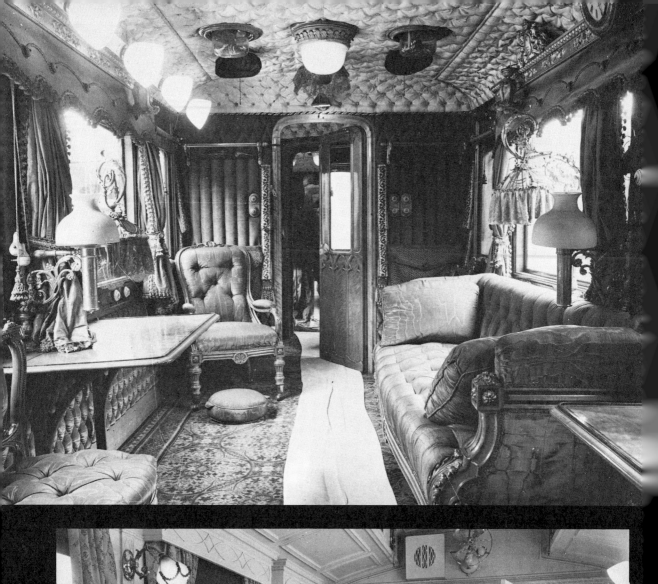

Compartments on two British royal trains: Opposite above: Queen Victoria's parlour. Opposite below: Edward VII's bedroom

Below: Peasants travelling in a third class railway carriage in France
Bottom: Leopold II, King of the Belgians, arriving on the Train Bleu on the Côte d'Azur

Below: Postcard celebrating the opening of the
Simplon tunnel, providing a railway link between
Italy and Switzerland in 1906
Bottom: Opening ceremony of the St Gotthard tunnel
in Switzerland, 1881

Opposite: A train on the rack-and-pinion railway
from Rocher de Naye in Switzerland

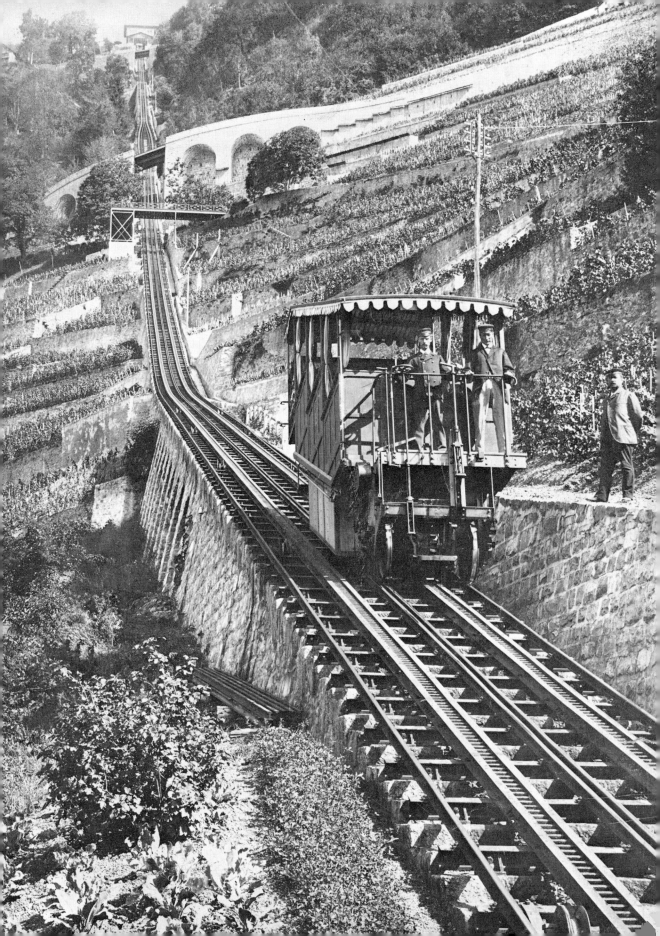

Left: Sirkedji Station in Istanbul: the terminus for the Orient Express
Below left: The Nordbahnhof in Vienna. Below: Turin Station

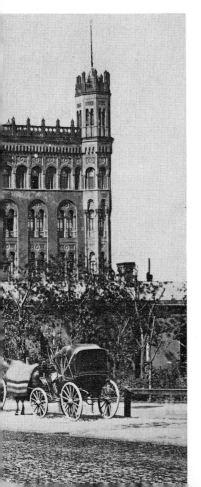

The transition from horse to motor in London at the turn of the century. Far left: A horse-drawn omnibus outside the National Gallery. Left: A motor omnibus in Regent Street

Below: Trams and cars in the Boulevard Victor Hugo, Nice

SAIL & STEAM
Ships and harbours

139

Previous pages: The Vieux Port at Marseilles, as
viewed from the Rue Canabière. Below: Quai du
Canal in Marseilles
Right: Bordeaux in 1895 with view of the river and
(below) the Quai de Bourgogne

Above left: The waterfront at Trondheim in Norway
Left: The harbour at Stockholm, with the
Riddarholm Church on the left and the roof of the
royal palace on the right
Above: The landing stage and the Steen at Antwerp

143

Two scenes of the waterfront at Hamburg. Bottom left: A forest of masts in the harbour. Bottom right: The Reimersfleth

Below: The royal palace in Budapest, viewed over the Danube

Brunel's *The Great Eastern*, launched in London in 1858
Below: *HMS Jumna*, a troopship being inspected at
Portsmouth by Queen Victoria

SS Titanic on her maiden voyage, 10 April 1912
Below: The Pool of London looking towards Tower
Bridge

AT WORK
Crafts and occupations

The Vintage. Opposite left: A portable boiler in the streets of Draguignan, Var, France. Left: Portuguese vineyard workers receiving their pay
Below: Offices of public letter writers outside the post office in Barcelona

Below: A group of tunny fishers on the French Riviera
Inset: Pulling in the nets in Naples harbour

Women at work. Opposite: A vendor of pottery cups asleep in a Naples street. Below: Cigar makers of Seville. Bottom: Workers rolling hand made cigarettes in a German factory

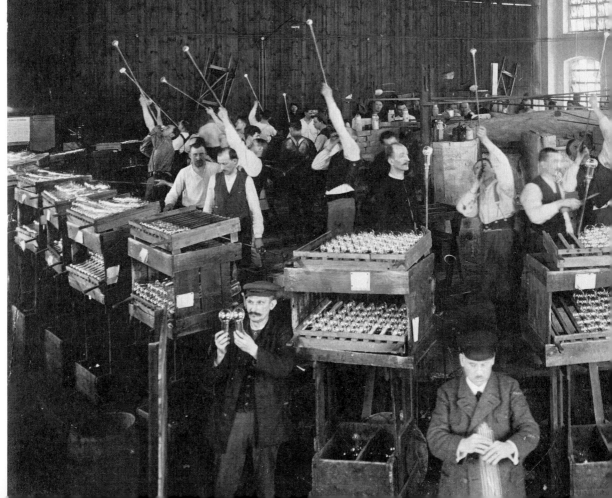

Above: Cooks in a German sausage factory
Opposite above: A German chimney sweep with his
assistant
Left: Lamp blowing in Germany

157

Below: A bootmaker at work in Dieppe, Normandy
Right: A Belgian woman pushing a coal truck at the
mouth of the pit at Charleroi
Inset: A milk inspector interrogating a vendor with her
dog cart in Belgium

Boot blacks cleaning the boots of
Bulgarian soldiers
Below: A man and his wife preparing
and spinning cloth in their home in
Bohemia

Right: A Polish chimney
sweep at work
Below right: A butcher's shop
in the working quarter of
Belgrade
Overleaf: Fisher-folk dividing
up their haul of fulmar on the
island of St Kilda, in the
Outer Hebrides

LEISURE & PLEASURE

Holidays, sport, entertainment

A Victorian summer picnic group, *c.* 1860. Right: A float at St Giles Fair in Oxford in 1885

Left: Prince Leopold of Bavaria shooting wild boar
Below: A meet of the Roman hunt at Monte Mario

Above: A Victorian river party, *c.* 1895. Below: Punting on the Thames in 1893

One of the highspots of the British summer season:
Henley Regatta in 1890

Below: A Danube steamer at its landing stage in Hungary

The expanding tourist industry. Below: Sightseers at Pompeii in the 1890s

Left: Intrepid hikers crossing the Chamonix glacier. Above: Mountaineers crossing a crevasse in the French Alps

A skiing party, which includes the Crown Princess of Sweden (third from right)

COUNTRY HOUSE PARTIES ON THE WATER: YACHTING SOCIETY AT COWES.

FAMOUS YACHT-OWNERS AND A TYPICAL RACE ON THE SOLENT.

Above: Olympic Games in London in 1908: the British team at the opening ceremony
Opposite above: Cowes Week, climax of the British summer season

Left: La Panhard et Levassor, driven by Levassor, winning the Paris-Bordeaux race in 1895

The British by the seaside. The central beach and esplanade at Blackpool in 1880. Inset: A family group in 1908 at Margate

Bathing beauties and machine at Ostende

The elegance of the Avenue Massena at Nice, just before the first world war.

Interior of a working-class *café chantant* in Seville

Below: *La Salle Touzet* in the Casino at Monte Carlo
Bottom: Basque peasants playing cards in the tap
room of an inn at Lemona in Spain

Sunday afternoon at the Tivoli Cafe overlooking Vienna
Night life in Paris. Below: The Moulin Rouge. Right: The Folies Bergère

Casque d'Or, a notorious woman *apache* from Paris

Opposite: A fashionable young English lady in bloomers
Below: Fisherwomen of Boulogne, France
Right: A fishwife from Aberdeen, Scotland

183

Before the comforts of piped water and domestic heating, women were obliged to wash their clothes in the river. Right: Icelandic housewives taking advantage of the natural hot springs. Below: Spanish women doing their laundry and collecting water from the river. Opposite below: A washing place in San Remo, Italy

Left: Turkish women in a silk factory at Broussa
Opposite below: Housemaids gathering at their
hiring place in Bucharest, ready for spring cleaning.

Last days in the Sultan's harem, 1906, before it was
dispersed. Below: A Circassian lady. Bottom: An
Ottoman harem lady

British women in action. Far left: Ironworkers in South Wales in 1865. Centre left: A housekeeper and her 'slaveys' in 1886. Below left: Shopgirls from a millinery establishment in 1899 on their Sunday outing. Left: Sweated industry: Women outworkers making frills for skirts, 1906. Below: Votes for women: Mrs Drummond addressing a crowd of men in Trafalgar Square, 1912

Soldiers in the Crimean War enjoying refreshment away from the battlefield. This photograph was taken by Roger Fenton during the spring or summer of 1855
Opposite: An Austrian field smithy during the war against France in Italy, 1859

WARS & WARRIORS
The armies of Europe

Inset: Crown Prince Frederick of Prussia inspecting
an infantry company of Prussian soldiers in 1858
Below: The Prussian army: a staged encounter with
the enemy, 1864

Below: A scene in the barracks of the Prussian life guards – the central depot for the wounded during the Austro-Prussian War, 1866

Above: Officers' wives of the Prussian life guards preparing bandages during the Austro-Prussian War, 1866
Below: Prussian military hospital near the Hasenheide, newly completed when this photograph was taken (1866)

Scenes in the Russo-Turkish War, 1877-8. Right:
Russian guard troops encamped at Tarem-Bourga in
Turkey. Below: Russian cossacks passing through a
Bulgarian village

War damage in Strasbourg in 1870, during the
Franco-Prussian War

French artillery on the Bouttes, Montmartre in Paris, 18 March 1871, just before the establishment of the Commune

Below: Austrian generals and general staff officers on
manoeuvres, 1893

Above: The Austro-Hungarian army on parade, *c.* 1885. On the left stands the Royal Hungarian Infantry, in the centre the Imperial Austrian Infantry, and on the right Austro-Hungarian sailors

Attempted reconciliation in 1894 between Prince Bismarck and Kaiser William II. Bismarck in Berlin with the Kaiser's brother, Prince Henry of Prussia

Scenes during the second Balkan War, 1913. Below:
Bulgarian troops entering a Serbian town. Bottom:
Bulgarian transport passing through a village in
Serbia. Opposite above: Bulgarians evacuating
Krushevo, Serbia. Opposite below: Guns on the old
fortifications overlooking the harbour at Durazzo in
Albania

Montenegran troops being reviewed at Cetinje in 1913. Below: Cavalry passing through Cetinje. Bottom: King Nicholas of Montenegro and Prince Alexander of Serbia inspecting troops. Opposite: Prince Mirko of Montenegro with an Austrian general at Cetinje

Crown Prince William of Prussia in the uniform of
the 2nd Cuirassiers with a detachment of Prussian
life guards, Potsdam 1912

Above: Crown Prince William leading Prussian foot guards, passing before the Kaiser

Below: Crown Prince William and officers of the 1st and 2nd Life Hussars, Danzig, *c.* 1910

Below: The four Prussian princes, in mitre caps and order sashes on the left of the photograph, taking part in 'Old Fritz's Day' in Potsdam in 1912

Right: Austrian dragoons march through the Heldenplatz, Vienna c. 1913
Bottom: Prussian Uhlans on manoeuvres

Previous pages: The Kaiser William II (third from left) awaiting a visit from the Russian royal family in the grounds of his new palace at Potsdam

Below: The 1st Foot guards march past the Kaiser during a parade on the Tempelhoferfelde, Berlin, c. 1912

Opposite below: Kaiser William II surrounded by his entourage at Potsdam

Bottom: The Kaiser on manoeuvres, talking to an Austrian general, while Lord Lonsdale, in the uniform of the Westmorland & Cumberland Yeomanry, looks on from the left

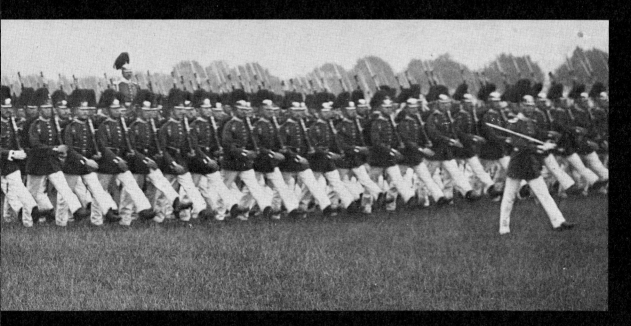

The British Army. Right:
Soldier of the Crimea. A piper of
the 42nd Highlanders, *c.* 1855.
Below: A trooper of the
Westmorland Yeomanry,
c. 1878

A British Ambassador with his military attaché and staff, *c.* 1885

THE FIRST OF NEW EUROPE
The children

Opposite: A young 'blood' from Southern Italy with two admirers. Above left: Prince Nicholas of Roumania in the costume of his Roman ancestors. Above right: A Serbian baby. Below: English family outing to the park, 1885

Opposite: Prince Gustaf Adolf of Sweden with his tricycle
Below: A child from the London slums

Right: The Kaiser (marked with an arrow) with his Empress and a group of poor children at the opening of a new home at Ahlbeck
Below: An open air school at Murcia in Spain
Below right: Lessons in a village school at Staphorst in Holland

THE LAMPS GO OUT

Europe goes to war

Young recruits on their way to be enlisted as volunteers to the German
army. Right: One of Kitchener's soldiers in camp, August 1914

The Western Front-graveyard of Old Europe. Stretcher-bearers in the mud

Nestle's Kindermehl
enthält
beste Schweizermilch.
Carl Schultz
616